The PRIVATE thoughts and prayers of:

Date:

Hi God, Let's Talk About MY LIFE

written by
Karen Ann Moore

illustrated by
Amy Wummer

Standard
PUBLISHING
CINCINNATI, OHIO

Scriptures quoted from the *International Children's Bible® New Century Version®*.
Copyright © 1986, 1988, 1999 by Tommy Nelson™, a division of Thomas Nelson, In,
Nashville, Tennessee 37214. Used by permission.

Published in association with the literary agency of Alive Communications, Inc.,
7680 Goddard Street, Suite 200, Colorado Springs, Colorado, 80920.

ISBN 0-7847-1246-8

09 08 07 06 05 04   9 8 7 6 5 4 3 2

Discover how cool it is to speak heart-to-heart with God.

1 Peter 5:7 reminds us to
Give all your worries to him, because he cares about you.

God cares and wants to hear about everything that happens in your life. How can you give all your worries to God? Through prayer.

But sometimes a question or a problem is so confusing that you don't know even how to begin to pray. That's when this book will help you!

Each part of this book looks at an issue or a difficult situation that kids—maybe even you—might have. All you have to do is turn to the situation that you're wondering about. You'll find out what the Bible says about that problem and some ideas about what to do.

Then pray. Let go of your worries. By writing out prayers in the journal sections of this book, you can hand your troubles over to God. Everything that you share with God in prayer brings you closer to him.

Choosing Right and Wrong

When you come to a traffic light on the road, red means stop and green means go. When it comes to life's issues, and choosing what to do, the signals aren't always that clear. A yellow light always means move with caution. That's a signal for prayer.

Friends and Fitting In

Remember what it was like when you were little and you were always the center of attention? Now you're no longer the most important person in the room. You have to go to school and make friends and fit in. Prayer can help you "work well with others."

Family Matters

Did you ever wonder how you ended up in your family? Family members can seem like crazy aliens from some other planet. Other times, they can be best friends who really understand you and support you. Praying about your family can help you learn to love them and live with them.

Finding Myself

You're learning new things, finding different interests, and there are so many new ways to look at life. It's not easy to figure out just who you are. Use prayer to find the answers to important questions like *Who am I? What do I really think? What do I really believe?*

A bunch of kids are going to hang out at the mall. My friend wants to go, but isn't allowed. He's planning to come to the mall anyway. He's going to lie to his mom and say that he's studying with me. He wants me to cover for him. I don't know what to say. I'm not really sure what to do.

signed,

Undercover Agent

MESSAGE TO GOD

God, I like my friend and I want to help, but I wonder if I should lie for him. I just want him to keep being my friend. Please help. Amen.

wHaT wOuld YoU Do?

❀ *Do it once, but tell him you won't do it again.*

❀ *Tell him how you feel about lying for him.*

❀ *Get some other opinions about what to do.*

❀ *Ground yourself for a day.*

Wow, this is a tough one! We all want to keep our friendships strong, but what happens when a friend asks a favor that's too big? What should you say when your friend asks you to lie for him?

Proverbs 12:17 says,
"An honest witness tells the truth, but a dishonest witness tells lies."

This simple verse points directly to the problem. By asking you to cover for him, your friend is asking you to tell a lie. If you go along with it, then you become a dishonest witness to the event in question. That's the reason you feel uncomfortable. The Holy Spirit in you is nudging you, asking you to consider your actions.

It may be pretty tempting to let it slide just this one time. Is it OK if you only do it once? If you think so, go back and read the Bible verse again! You'll feel better, and you'll be doing what's right, if you speak the truth to your friend. Tell him how you feel about covering up. If your friend asks why being honest is so important to you, take that chance to share about your relationship with Jesus.

You may find a time when it's important for someone's safety or protection to cover up for them. If that's the case, talk to your parents before you do anything!

Decisions like this have a way of building character. Even adults—probably even your parents!—deal with this issue, so ask them for advice. Above all, pray about it. Ask God to guide you and to help you to be an honest witness.

MESSAGE TO GOD

God, help me be an honest witness. Help me speak the truth to my friend and be strong enough not to cover up when I know in my heart it's wrong. Help me to do what is right in your sight. Amen.

Prayer Starters

God, I covered up for my friend when he ...

God, I need help making a decision about ...

God, help me to tell the truth all the time.
Help me to be honest about . . .

God, today I will be honest in everything I
do. I will speak the truth. Amen.

What God did to help me to be honest . . .

What I plan to do next time . . .

I was chatting with a friend on the phone, and she told me that another friend of ours had stolen a CD from the store. I couldn't believe it, but I didn't defend my friend. I just accepted the story and the next day, I told someone else. It turned out my friend didn't steal anything. I wish I had kept my mouth shut.

signed,
Big Mouth

MESSAGE TO GOD

God, I feel bad.
Sometimes I do such stupid,
unkind things. I wouldn't
want anyone to say things
about me that weren't true.
Please help. Amen.

WHaT wOUld YoU Do?

❀ Promise to eat liver if you ever gossip again.

❀ Apologize to your friend.

❀ Start a Gossips Anonymous group.

❀ Become a gossip columnist.

When you listen to an unkind story about someone else—whether it's true or not—you are gossiping.

Proverbs 26:22 says,
"The words of a gossip are like tasty bits of food; people like to gobble them up."

People like to hear juicy tidbits of gossip. Listening to stories about others can seem yummy if it makes you feel glad to be "in the know." Maybe it makes you feel better about yourself because you didn't do that weird thing. Gossip can be like a big dessert table where we love to get the best cookies before someone else does.

What if you did not gobble up gossip? When someone is telling a story about another person, and you know it's hurtful or might not be true, or it's none of your business, then DON'T listen! Just walk away! Tell yourself, "I'm not interested in gossip." You could pretend you're on a gossip diet. "No thanks, I'm trying to quit."

If you do hear some gossip, then do NOT pass it on.

Proverbs 26:20 says,
"Without wood, a fire will go out, and without
gossip, quarreling will stop."

What happens when we're out of wood? Well, the fire goes out. That means if we don't add more stories to a gossip session, the gossiping will stop.

So what should someone who gossiped do? The first choice was to eat liver if you ever gossip again. OK, this might work, but liver is just too gross for words. Instead, you could apologize to your friend. Whew! This is the hardest choice on the list. Telling someone that you did something wrong is hard. Asking for forgiveness is hard. But putting out the fire, stopping the flow of gossip, and being kind to your friends are all good choices.

MESSAGE TO GOD

Dear God, Sometimes I eat up gossip and pass it along to someone else. I know that's unkind and none of my business. You don't want me to do it. Help me go on a gossip diet. Amen.

Prayer Starters

God, I need to ask forgiveness because I gossiped about...

I remember when someone gossiped about me and how I felt. It happened like this...

God, help me to stick to my gossip diet.
Remind me to . . .

God, I am happy to go on a gossip diet. I know I feel much better when I do not eat up gossip. Amen.

What I did . . .

How God answered my prayer . . .

I like my friends at school, but sometimes they're rude to other kids. Last week Sarah came up and started talking to us. I talked to her, but no one else did. My friends acted like Sarah didn't belong there. I didn't like it, but I didn't really do anything about it. I don't want to lose my friends, but I want to be Sarah's friend, too. Do I have to choose?

signed,

Friendly Me

MESSAGE TO GOD

```
God, I feel kind of lousy.
I kind of get the idea from
my friends that other kids
don't fit in our group. I
don't really get that.
Please help. Amen.
```

WHaT wOUld YOU Do?

❀ *Make friends with everyone.*

❀ *Only make friends with the "in" crowd.*

❀ *Decide it's not really your problem.*

1 John 3:18, 19 says,

"We should love people not only with words and talk, but by our actions and true caring. This is the way we know that we belong to the way of truth."

You know enough about Jesus to see his example; he was kind to the poor and unpopular and wasn't worried about being part of the "in" crowd. Just like Jesus, you should share friendship with the popular kids and the unpopular ones.

It's right to show friendship and compassion to everyone.

It's great that you so sincerely want to be a friend. The problem here is that one of your friends has decided for you who is and who is not worthy of your friendship. Being unkind to someone to please the "in" crowd isn't the best choice. Ignoring the issue or deciding it's not your problem won't make you feel better, either. Now you have to decide whether to do the "popular" thing, or the right thing.

Going against the crowd can be a very hard thing to do! But you're not the only one who's had to make this kind of choice. A good example of this from the Bible is Daniel. The book of Daniel tells us of the times Daniel's right choices made him *very* unpopular (Read Daniel 3 and Daniel 6).

There will be other times in your life when you have to make the same kind of choice. Each time you have to decide between doing what's popular and doing what's right, pray for God's help and let his Holy Spirit guide you. Choosing what you know is right—whether it's popular or not—sets your heart at peace. It's the peace that God gives when you do his will.

Popular

MESSAGE TO GOD

God, you know how complicated friendships can be. Help me not to worry about being popular. Instead, I want to be the friend you want me to be. Thanks, God. Amen.

Prayer Starters

God, I don't want to lose my friends...

God, I have a problem that's tricky because...

God, the popular thing and the right thing aren't the same in this situation . . .

God, today I am going to be caring toward everyone. I don't care how popular others are or how popular I am. Thanks. Amen.

Here's how I chose to do the right thing even though it was unpopular with my friends . . .

How I think God helped me . . .

Names of friends who help me do what's right . . .

My friend just took up smoking. It really bothers me, but I can't seem to get her to stop. I don't want anyone to think I smoke. She says it's none of my business, but I know it's not good for her.

signed,
No Smoking, Please

MESSAGE TO GOD

Dear God, I am worried about my friend. I know that what she's doing isn't good for her. Please help me know what to do. Amen.

wHaT wOUld YoU Do?

- ❀ Figure it's not really your business.
- ❀ Tell someone you trust.
- ❀ Cough a lot when you're around smokers.
- ❀ Flush the cigarettes down the toilet.

Even though the Bible doesn't exactly say "Don't smoke!" it does remind us that our bodies are special dwelling places for God's Holy Spirit.

1 Corinthians 6:19, 20 says,
"You should know that your body is a temple for the Holy Spirit who is in you. You have received the Holy Spirit from God. So you do not belong to yourselves, because you were bought by God for a price. So honor God with your bodies."

We can honor God with our bodies by feeling good about ourselves and working to be healthy. We should do our best to keep our bodies in top working order. Smoking, drinking, or drugs won't make us healthy or provide a good place for God's Spirit to dwell.

It doesn't really matter where you go to school; sooner or later someone you know will begin to smoke or try drinking or do some other harmful thing to her body. It's not easy to know

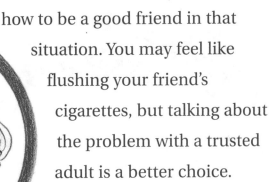

how to be a good friend in that situation. You may feel like flushing your friend's cigarettes, but talking about the problem with a trusted adult is a better choice.

Of course, keep praying for your friend. Pray that God will show her the harm she's doing and that God will help her to stop.

Smoking makes you sick! It stunts your growth and turns your teeth and fingernails yellow. It also can cause cancer of the lungs, mouth, and throat. For more information about quitting smoking, contact the American Lung Association at 1-800-LUNGUSA or e-mail them at TATU@lungusa.org.

MESSAGE TO GOD

Dear God, I know I belong to you. Help me to honor you with my body. Thank you. Amen.

Prayer Starters

God, I don't know what to say to my friend, but I think I might say . . .

God, please help me and my friend to like our bodies enough to take care of them by . . .

God, sometimes I feel pressured to . . .

God, I will take care of my body as you want me to. Please help my friends take care of themselves, too. Help all my friends who smoke. Amen.

What I did about my friend . . .

What God did to answer my prayer . . .

Some of my friends have traveled a lot and visited places all over the world. I've never been anyplace. For some reason, when they asked where I had been, I said I hadn't been to any other countries yet, but that we were going in the summer. The problem is, we're not going anywhere. I just didn't want them to know my family can't afford those things.

signed,
Wish I'd Told the Truth

God, the truth is, well, I didn't tell the truth and now I feel upset about it. Is there such a thing as an OK lie? Please help me understand this stuff better. Amen.

wHaT woUld YoU Do?

- ❀ *Make yourself stand in the corner.*
- ❀ *Read a book about another country.*
- ❀ *Tell your friends the truth.*
- ❀ *Wash your mouth out with soap for lying.*

It's easy to fall into the trap of thinking that telling a little fib isn't the same thing as a lie. Maybe you tell a friend that you love her new spiked hairdo—but you really don't. Maybe you pretend to like Grandma's fruitcake—but you really think it's terrible. You'll find this issue keeps coming up, so it's important to decide how you should handle it.

Proverbs 21:2 tells us,
"You may believe you are doing right, but the Lord judges your reasons."

A lie is always a lie—even if it's just a little one meant to save someone's feelings or meant to help you save face. Even a little lie can trap you into a bad situation. (How much gross fruitcake are you willing to eat because you weren't truthful?) Telling the truth makes you free to be the person you really are. If your actions prick your conscience, then you aren't free.

*The true you is the you
to share with your friends.*

If you catch yourself fibbing, washing your mouth out with soap won't make you come clean. You have to decide on the inside that being truthful is more important than saving face. When in doubt, tell the truth.

Tell God about your problem in prayer. Keeping your mouth under control is one of the hardest things to do! Resolve to say a quick, silent prayer for help whenever you feel a lie about to come out. God will help you.

MESSAGE TO GOD

Dear God, forgive me for when I didn't tell the truth. Help me remember the best thing for everyone is to speak the truth. Thank you for looking into my heart to judge what I do. Amen.

Prayer Starters

God, I told a lie about...

God, I know that someone lied to me about...

God, thanks for helping me tell the truth to . . .

Today, God, I will do my best to tell the truth. When I don't know just what to say, I will pray for help. Amen.

Something I told the truth about even though it was hard is . . .

What God did to help . . .

I've had the same best friend for three years. We do everything together. We talk on the phone all the time. We even go on vacation with each other's families. But, lately, my friend has stopped calling me every day. We don't seem to do as much together. I don't understand what is going on.

signed,
Drifting Apart

MESSAGE TO GOD

Dear God, I don't understand what is going on with my best friend. I liked it the way it was. My feelings are really hurt. Please help me figure out what to do. Amen.

WHat wOuld YoU Do?

- ❀ Get someone to ask your friend what is wrong.

- ❀ Ask your friend what is wrong.

- ❀ Ask your goldfish what is wrong.

- ❀ Eat lots of chocolate!

Friendship is an important part of our lives and God understands how much we need it. Sometimes a friendship slips away or changes. Friends who were once very close sometimes grow apart. That can hurt. If your friend doesn't want to keep your relationship close, you can't control that. But you can control the way you handle the situation.

The Bible offers advice for how to treat your friend—no matter what is going on in the friendship.

1 Corinthians 13:5-7 says,
"Love is not rude, is not selfish, and does not get upset with others. Love does not count up wrongs that have been done. Love is not happy with evil but is happy with the truth. Love patiently accepts all things. It always trusts, always hopes, and always remains strong."

Read the verse again. This time, replace the word love with the words *a friend*. What a good friend you are!

What else can you do? Getting someone else to find out what your other friend is thinking doesn't usually work. Your pet could make you feel better and so could a nice box of chocolates, but the best thing is to be patient with your friend and find a way to talk. You've been friends a long time. You've learned how to talk. You can talk about this, too. Whether you decide to stay best friends, or you decide to move on to making new friends, talking about it will make you both feel better.

You and God can be working on your problem together. He knows how to help. Use prayer as a tool for making things better.

Dear God, thank you for the good friendship advice in 1 Corinthians. Please help my friend and me to talk things out. Amen.

Prayer Starters

God, I'm afraid I lost my friend. That makes me feel . . .

God, help me trust you in this situation . . .

God, I really want my friend back because . . .

My prayer for my friend is . . .

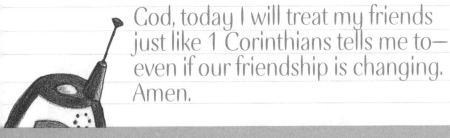

God, today I will treat my friends just like 1 Corinthians tells me to—even if our friendship is changing. Amen.

What I did to work this out with my friend . . .

What God did to help me . . .

Our friendship is . . .

Over the summer, my best friend moved to another city. I miss her a lot. I feel a little lonely at school without her. We always used to sit together at lunch and we'd hang out after school. I know I need to make new friends, but it's hard for me. I just wish my friend was still with me. What should I do?

signed,

Need a Friend

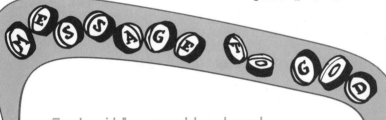

God, it's pretty hard being without my best friend. Would you help me to find new friends? Thanks. Amen.

WHaT wOuld YoU Do?

- ❀ Join an after school club.

- ❀ Make it a point to talk to one new person a day at school.

- ❀ Get a job as a volunteer.

- ❀ Join a group at church.

It's never easy to try new things. Whether you're trying a new activity, or a new friendship, it takes some courage and some faith to do it.

One first step in making a new friend is getting up the courage to talk to someone new. That's why joining a club or working as a volunteer is such a great way to make friends—there you automatically have something to talk about!

When you're having an especially lonely day at school, or when you're thinking about talking to someone new, remember God is with you. Pray to him right then. He promises to help you.

Proverbs 3:5, 6 says,

"Trust the Lord with all your heart, and don't depend on your own understanding. Remember the Lord in all you do, and he will give you success."

Now that's a great promise! You can trust God's love and good will for your life. Trust the Lord to keep you from feeling lost and lonely. Depend on him to help you build new friendships. You can also trust that God hears you when you go to him in prayer.

Don't forget about your old friend who has moved away. She's going through the same struggle you are! You can pray for each other. Write your friend a letter and share some tips for making new friends. Remember you're not alone. The Lord will help you be successful.

MESSAGE TO GOD

Dear God, thank you for being with me and with my friend as we both try to make new friends. Help us keep our friendship, too. I know that with your help, new friends will soon come into both of our lives. Amen.

Prayer Starters

God, I'm nervous about making new friends because …

God, help me be willing to try to make new friends …

God, I think I might try to be friends with . . .

Today, God, I trust in you as I try to create some new friendships. I thank you for being with me and loving me so much. Amen.

What I did to find new friends . . .

What God did to help me find new friends . . .

Here are the names of new friends I reached out to . . .

I really like this very cool kid at school. This is my first time liking someone who seems to like me right back, and now I'm not quite sure how to act. I'm sure nobody else would think this was very important because I'm just a kid, but it is important to me. Does God help with stuff like this?

signed,
Wondering Heart

MESSAGE TO GOD

Dear God, I really like this boy at school and he likes me, too. Please help me to be myself and know how to act. Amen.

WHaT wOUld YoU Do?

❀ Just have fun.

❀ Think back about other "firsts" in your life and how you worked things out.

❀ Get a little advice from family and friends you trust.

It's fun to know that you have someone special in your life. Relationships help you learn to listen and care, to share your ideas and your thoughts, and to accept other people's ideas and thoughts. God will be with you in all your friendships and more serious relationships as you grow. Here's a verse that might guide and encourage you in this new relationship.

1 Timothy 4:12 says,
"Do not let anyone treat you as if you are unimportant because you are young. Instead, be an example to the believers with your words, your actions, your love, your faith, and your pure life."

Do you like me? Circle one. Yes No Maybe

As with everything else in your life, God is with you now. He will bless your friendship and guide you as long as you keep asking for his help. Matters of the heart are always a bit tricky, but just enjoy this time in your life and see what you learn from it and what you can bring to it. All of your relationships give you ways to honor God by your actions.

Pray and ask God to help you to always honor him in this special friendship.

MESSAGE TO GOD

Dear God, please bless my friendship. Help me to listen each day for your guidance. Thank you for giving me this very special friend. Amen.

Prayer Starters

God, I'm so excited about . . .

God, help me just have fun . . .

Dear God, please guide me in this new
relationship with . . .

Dear God, I am learning to trust
you more in all that I do. Thank you
for blessing me with my special
friend. Amen.

How I figured out the best way to act . . .

Here's what God did to help me . . .

I've liked the same person at school for a while. Finally we started liking each other and it's been great. Only, things changed. We broke up last week. Mom says it's just part of relationships and growing up, but that doesn't really help. It feels so weird at school. I just want to hide when I see him in the hall.

signed,
Feeling Blue

MESSAGE TO GOD

God, please help! I feel so stupid at school now and I don't like that everyone knows I've been dumped. I know I'm just a kid, but I liked this person. Amen.

WHaT wOuld YoU Do?

- ✿ Talk to friends about it.
- ✿ Get a new pet goldfish.
- ✿ Start a new hobby.
- ✿ Feel your feelings.

Letting go of someone you really care about is hard. Time is usually the thing that helps you to heal. Until then, you can trust that God cares about how you feel.

With time, you'll probably be friends again with the person who was so special to you. In fact, at this time in your life, it's good to move on as quickly as you can. Staying involved with school activities, church youth groups, and hobbies you enjoy will help the time pass. Before you know it, you'll find someone else likes you or you like someone else. In the meantime, remember that God knows your heart and wants to comfort you.

2 Corinthians 1:3, 4 says,

"God is the Father who is full of mercy and all comfort. He comforts us every time we have trouble, so when others have trouble, we can comfort them with the same comfort God gives us. "

Everyone handles disappointment differently. Talking to friends can be helpful (though if you've ever read the book of Job, you may want to be careful about what friends you talk to!). Getting a new pet might bring some joy into your life, but of course, that's not always an option. Starting a new hobby or picking up on an old one might also be good. Exercise helps, too. Probably the best thing is simply to feel what you feel, let some time pass and then seek God's comfort and his help. He will share this time with you and bring you peace.

Dear God, thank you
for caring about my problem.
I can find comfort in you.
Amen.

Prayer Starters

God, thanks for helping me through this hard time . . .

God, help me bless my friend . . .

My feelings were really hurt when . . .

God, even though I'm sad, I am
trusting today in your comfort and
believing you will help me get
through this disappointment. Amen.

What I did to help myself feel better . . .

What God did to help me . . .

What I learned about relationships . . .

I hate it when people act like they're your friends sometimes, but other times they ignore you or treat you badly. For example, my friend Tim seems to be around whenever I get a new computer game. Then, when he gets bored with it, I don't see him again for weeks. I think that's so rude! I hope I never treat any of my friends like that.

signed,

A Friend All the Time

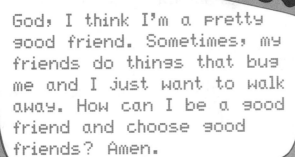

MESSAGE TO GOD

God, I think I'm a pretty good friend. Sometimes, my friends do things that bug me and I just want to walk away. How can I be a good friend and choose good friends? Amen.

WHAT WOULD YOU DO?

✿ Just be friends with turtles.

✿ Send your friend to "cool" school.

✿ Do your best and know you won't always get it right.

✿ Tell yourself you don't need friends anyway.

We can't always figure out why someone acts like a friend sometimes and then doesn't other times. That kind of person is a fair-weather friend. Fair-weather friends are only around when things are good. But when the skies turn gray and the good times are gone, they walk away and look for someone else to hang with. Rain or shine, we need good friends.

The question is, what kind of friends are good to have, and what kind of friend does God want you to be?

Proverbs 18:24 says,
"Some friends may ruin you, but a real friend will be more loyal than a brother."

The Bible gives fair-weather friends two thumbs down. According to this verse, real friends are loyal. They stay by you like family on days when you're having fun with a computer game, and on days that aren't very fun.

Now you know what kind of friend you DON'T want to have or be. Think about what kind of friend you DO want to be. Real friends are kind, thoughtful, fun to be with, and make you feel good about yourself. The Golden Rule says to treat others as you want to be treated yourself. Good friends do that.

The Bible offers several stories about truly beautiful friendships that you might want to read. The story of Ruth and Naomi is in the book of Ruth, or you can read about the friendship between Jonathan and David in 1 Samuel.

Even the best of friends disappoint each other sometimes. But most of the time, friends laugh together, lighten up dull situations, and make anything look better. Just be yourself and share your heart. You'll be someone other people like to be around. That makes you a pretty cool friend.

MESSAGE TO GOD

Dear God, thanks for my good friends. Help me be loyal and show kindness in all the things I do. Thanks for helping me to become a better friend. Amen.

Prayer Starters

God, thanks for reminding me to help my friend by . . .

Dear God, I forgot the Golden Rule when I . . .

God, My friends are great because . . .

God, I was disappointed in my friend when . . .

God, I want to be a good friend always.
I want to be a true, loyal friend. Amen.

These are the things I've decided to do to help me be a better
friend . . .

Here's one of the answers to my prayer about friends . . .

This kid, Josh, makes nasty remarks all the time. I've heard him call kids fat, or dumb, or stupid. It just doesn't stop. I want to tell him off, but I never quite know what to say. I've seen kids walk away crying from those remarks. It makes me mad even though he hasn't said anything right to my face.

signed,

Bugged by a Bully

MESSAGE TO GOD

God, some people seem mad at the world and they take it out on anybody that walks by. What should I do? Is there anything you can do? Please help. Amen

WHaT wOuld YoU Do?

✿ Post "No Bullying Without a License" signs around the school.

✿ Ignore him.

✿ See if a teacher can help.

✿ Try to get to know him.

Not everyone is nice. Not everyone even tries to be nice. Josh and other bullies like him don't seem to know how to treat people. Their meanness is so hard to take!

Sometimes there is a reason why bullies hurt other people. Maybe Josh puts others down because he doesn't feel very good about himself. But no matter why they may be doing it, people who think up evil plans or hurt others are not living as God wants.

If a bully at your school makes serious threats (like bringing a gun to school), tell an adult.

It's hard to deal with a mean person. Posting "stop bullying" signs probably won't work. Ignoring him may not be the ticket either. But there is a right way to deal with someone like Josh.

The Bible tells us what Jesus says about how we should treat each other.

Matthew 5:44 says,
"Love your enemies. Pray for those who hurt you."

What a hard thing to do! You may be boiling with anger because a bully has hurt you or your friends, but Jesus wants you to be kind to him. You could be kind by saying "hello" to him (that takes bravery!). You could be kind by finding a way to include him in something so you can get to know him. He may just need to feel someone cares about him, and your kindness could make a difference.

Your kindness may or may not be returned. You may not be able to change the bully, but you can pray for him. Pray that the bully will know God loves him. Pray that God will help the bully to stop hurting others. God has the power to help this situation.

Pray. Be kind.
Be an example of kindness.
God will bless you.

MESSAGE TO GOD

Dear God, please help me and people at school to treat each other with kindness. Help bullies to give up hurting others and become more of what you would have them be. Thanks. Amen.

Prayer Starters

God, I'm tired of being bullied . . .

God, when someone is mean to me, I feel . . .

God, help me to treat others with kindness. Amen.

What I did about . . .

What God did to help . . .

What I'll do the next time I face a bully . . .

I feel really lucky that I have special talents. I know God gave them to me and that's really cool. One of my talents is acting. I love to be in musicals so I can sing and dance. I'd like to get my friend to try out for the next play. She says she'd be too afraid. What can I do to encourage her? I want to help.

signed,
Talent Scout

MESSAGE TO GOD

God, thanks for blessing me with my own talents. I enjoy using them. I like that other people enjoy what I do. Help me to encourage my friend to try out her own talents, too. Amen.

wHaT woUld YoU Do?

❀ Figure out what your friend does best.

❀ Take your friend to the next play at a community theatre.

❀ Make up a play at home and videotape it for fun.

❀ Do something your friend is good at, but you're not.

Every person has talents—or things they're good at—which are gifts from God. It's great to recognize your talents and use them. You're so kind to want to encourage your friend to try out her own God-given talents.

This short verse from Proverbs is a nice reminder about what friends can do for each other.

Proverbs 27:17 says,
"As iron sharpens iron, so people can improve each other."

People really can improve each other. One of the fun parts of friendship comes from helping each other try new things. Plus, sharing time together in special ways makes your friendship stronger.

Of course, not everybody has a talent for the same activity. If you have a talent for acting, your friend's talent might be for singing or something different. Figure out together what she's good at. If you both want to do plays, go to some shows and talk about them. If she's too nervous to hit the stage, maybe your friend could work behind the scenes.

Keep in mind that there are things your friend can do that you probably feel uncertain about trying, too. Maybe you should try something your friend does well.

If your friend doesn't try out for the play, share the things you do have in common. Encourage each other in other things you do well . . . and in the things you don't do well.

Always be thankful to God for his blessings of talents.

Our talents

MESSAGE TO GOD

Dear God, thank you for the talents you've given me. And thank you for my friend and her talents, too. Help us to use our talents for you. Amen.

Prayer Starters

Cod, I'm thankful that I'm good at ...

Help me encourage my friend to ...

Help me with things I'm NOT good at such as ...

God, I am thankful for the gifts you have given me. I will do my best to be a good and encouraging friend. Amen.

What I did to encourage my friend . . .

What God did to answer my prayer . . .

What I learned about friendship . . .

My family isn't perfect. We get mad at each other and we say mean things sometimes. But most of the time we help each other, and in our own ways, we love each other. We're not like a "perfect" family, but we're OK. What's the best way to get past the times when I'm mad at my family?

signed,

Family Kid

MESSAGE TO GOD

God, I'm thankful for my family. They make me crazy now and then, but most of the time, they're pretty good. Help me be someone who makes our family better. Amen.

WHaT wOUld YoU Do?

- ✿ Create special time to be with each member of your family.
- ✿ Tell jokes to make them laugh.
- ✿ Be the first one to forgive when there's a problem.
- ✿ Print a T-shirt that says "Blessed with a great family!"

*H*ow wonderful it is to be part of a loving, happy home. You're right to feel blessed and thankful. But there are times when even close family members get on each other's nerves!

Ephesians 4:32 says,
"Be kind and loving to each other, and forgive each other just as God forgave you in Christ."

You can help keep your family strong by always showing your mom and dad and brothers and sisters kindness. The Bible verse also asks you to forgive. Forgiveness is an important key to most of life's relationships—especially in a family. Sometimes you might feel disappointed or let down by your family. It's at those times, when you probably don't feel like forgiving or loving, that you need to love and forgive your family the most!

The choices list suggests carving out time for each other. Even family members may not know each other well. Taking time with members of your family is a great way to strengthen each other. So, go to the movies, read books, play games, exercise, make pizza, talk over the church sermon—do whatever it takes to be together. It'll be great!

Telling good jokes could make you a hit at home. However, if stand-up comedy is not your thing, try other ways to entertain the folks at your house. Happy families find lots of ways to laugh together.

In all things, pray to God and thank him for your family. A strong family is a blessing from God. He will help you find ways to love and strengthen your family even more.

MESSAGE TO GOD

Dear God, thanks for giving me such an awesome family. When we have a fight, help me be the first to forgive. Help me be more like you and share your love with everyone in my own home. Amen.

Prayer Starters

God, I'm not feeling very loving today. I feel …

God, let me tell you more about my family …

God, I need to forgive someone in my family because . . .

Today, God, I'll be a great member of my family. I'll be more like the person you want me to be. Amen.

What I did to be a more forgiving member of my family . . .

What God did to help me . . .

My prayers for my family . . .

M y parents are so protective. That's OK most of the time, but sometimes it bugs me. For example, one of my friends is planning a party. Because my friend is older than me, mom and dad won't let me go to the party. They said they like my friend, but I'm too young for house parties. Why do they treat me like a baby? Don't they trust me?

signed,
Too Young

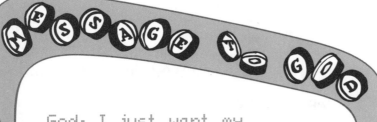

MESSAGE TO GOD

God, I just want my parents to let me grow up. Sometimes they are too protective. Please help! Amen.

wHaT wOUld YOU Do?

❀ Forget about the party, but mope a lot.

❀ Obey your parents.

❀ Whine a lot.

❀ Invite your parents to the party.

You didn't come into the world with a "how to" book. Since you were born, your parents have been feeding you, making sure you were healthy, and doing their best to provide for all your needs. Getting you to grow up is a process that takes some work on both sides. You can help your parents help you by respecting the choices they make for you now.

Deuteronomy 5:16 says,
"Honor your father and your mother as the Lord your God has commanded you. Then you will live a long time, and things will go well for you."

One key to understanding what to do is in the word *honor.* It may seem old-fashioned, but honor means to give respect. Think of the people you really respect and why you respect them. The Bible tells us that when we give honor to those in authority (like our parents), things go well for us.

There's nothing wrong with wanting to go to a party or trying to find ways to discuss something with your parents. It's natural for you to want to branch out into new things with more responsibility (like going to parties) as you grow up. You can plead your case to your parents in a respectful way, but moping around and whining aren't right. In the end, if you and your parents don't agree about something, obeying your parents' wishes is the right thing to do.

But keep praying. Ask God to help you honor your parents and ask him to give your parents wisdom in making decisions about what's best for you. Maybe they'd agree to having a party at your house.

Dear God, please help me honor my parents. Sometimes it is so tempting to sneak away and disobey. Please help us find ways to talk about these things in the future. Amen.

Prayer Starters

God, I just don't understand why my parents won't let me ...

God, please help me find a way to talk to my parents about ...

God, here's how I might show my parents I'm growing up . . .

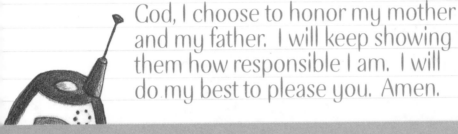

God, I choose to honor my mother and my father. I will keep showing them how responsible I am. I will do my best to please you. Amen.

What God did to help me . . .

It was really a good choice to . . .

Sometimes I get along with my brother, but sometimes I don't. I like my privacy, and I don't like anyone getting into my things without permission. Mom says that's fine, but my brother doesn't respect that. He comes into my room and "borrows" things without asking. I don't know if God cares about stuff like this, but I hope he does!

signed,

Bugged by a Brother

MESSAGE TO GOD

```
God, my brother bugs me.
He acts like my feelings
don't matter. Please help me
deal with him in a way that
pleases you. Amen.
```

What would You Do?

- ❀ Bribe your brother with cookies.

- ❀ "Borrow" things from him and don't give them back for a while.

- ❀ Ask your friends for advice.

- ❀ Follow him around and be annoying till he asks you to go away.

Brothers and sisters can be such a pain! When they don't respect your privacy or your feelings, it's frustrating. You can't control what others do—that's not your job! But you can control your own actions.

The Bible records that familiar verse you learned as the Golden Rule.

Luke 6:31 says,
"Do to others what you would want them to do to you."

Does this mean you have to let your brother just take your stuff? No. You still can set up your boundaries. For example, a boundary you could set up would be "Please don't borrow something without asking me first." The difference is in how you choose to handle it when your brother messes up. Jesus reminds us to treat others as we want to be treated—with kindness and patience.

So what are you going to choose to do? Getting cookies and bribing your brother might be a fun way to make your point. Maybe he doesn't realize how seriously you want him to leave your things alone. It could be a sweet way to show you mean what you say.

"Borrowing" things from him that you don't give back is giving your brother a taste of his own medicine, but it's not very kind. It's certainly not treating your brother the same way you want to be treated.

The best thing you can do is to treat your brother as you want him to treat you. It will take some patience, so pray for God's help in doing this. It won't hurt to pray for God to help your brother follow the Golden Rule himself.

MESSAGE TO GOD

Dear God, it still bugs me that my brother doesn't leave my things alone. Help me to trust that you are working on this problem with me. Show me what you would have me do. Amen.

Prayer Starters

God, I feel like screaming when ...

Hi, God, hope you heard my prayer about ...

God, please help my brother to see that it upsets me when he does this . . .

Dear God, I know you love me and are aware of things that bug me. Help my siblings and me to follow the Golden Rule. Amen.

What I did to help this situation . . .

What God did . . .

What I would do differently . . .

I'm so shy. I just don't seem to fit anywhere at school. I'm too shy to try out for the band or sports. I want to, but I just can't. There was a dance at school and my friend wanted to go, so I went, too. I stood by the door most of the time so I could run out at the first chance. I didn't dance. I didn't even talk to anyone. Will I ever get over this?

signed,
Too Shy

MESSAGE TO GOD

God, I feel so dopey.
I have a hard time making
friends and talking to people.
I want to have more fun, but
I can't quite make myself do
it. Please help me to be
brave! Amen.

Shy Girl's 'To Do' List

❀ *Practice saying nice things to yourself in front of a mirror.*

❀ *Get friends to help you.*

❀ *Reward yourself for any effort you make.*

❀ *Write down three things that block you from making friends.*

Lots of kids are too timid (that's another word for shy) to try out for sports or join clubs. Shyness is a kind of fear; someone who's shy doesn't quite trust that the world will be fair or good to her. When we let those fears keep us from making friends or joining cool activities, we're really missing out! It takes some effort, but you can overcome your shyness and even replace it with self-confidence.

It always helps to talk a problem over with friends. Don't be afraid to be honest about it. Good friends will help calm your fears and encourage you to go for it at a band tryout or the next school dance!

Make it a goal to do one new thing or talk to one new person per week—something that you might have thought you were too shy to try. Always reward yourself for trying.

It may help to write about your situation. Use your journal to face the things that block you from making friends or joining groups. Sometimes just seeing your fears written down can make them seem smaller.

Christians have a special advantage for overcoming shyness. The Bible helps to explain why this is true.

2 Timothy 1:7 says,
"God did not give us a spirit that makes us afraid but a spirit of power and love and self-control."

As Christians, we have God's spirit within us. That spirit is strong and powerful—strong enough to help us overcome the things that hold us back. You can talk to new friends. You can try out for the team. Try not to be too hard on yourself and remember that wonderful power that God has put inside you to help you every single day.

MESSAGE TO GOD

Dear God, you've given me a spirit that is strong and powerful. Help me to use it so I won't be so shy. Amen.

Prayer Starters

I don't like being shy because . . .

My shy side couldn't do it again, God, but I felt so brave when I . . .

Please help me talk to . . .

God, today I'm going to make one effort to be less shy. I might just take a baby step, but I know you're with me, so I'm going to try. Amen.

Three things that keep me from trying harder are . . .

The first effort I made was . . .

How God helped me . . .

My friend is so much prettier than I am. She's taller and she has blond hair. I think I look weird. Another friend is pretty, too, and she has the coolest clothes. I feel like a reject from a charity shop. I wish I could be cool, but I can't afford the latest stuff from the mall. I just feel dorky.

signed,

Ugly Duckling

God, I feel like the ugly duckling. I don't think I'm a swan in hiding. I'm just a duck. I wish I were someone else—someone better looking, that is. Please help me. Amen.

WHaT wOUld YoU Do?

❀ Look for the flaws in your friends.

❀ Never look in a mirror again.

❀ Consider all the things that are special about you.

❀ Dye your hair purple and pink so you really stand out.

Sometimes we look at our friends' clothes or hair and we feel like we don't measure up. Commercials on TV and models in magazines tell us that beauty is being a certain size, or a certain hair color, or wearing a certain brand. Sometimes we think we're supposed to look like the models in the ads.

We all worry about how we look. Who doesn't want to be beautiful? The real question is, what is beautiful? God says there is something more to beauty than having the best hair and always wearing the latest styles. God is concerned about the beauty of our hearts.

1 Samuel 16:7 says,
   "God does not see the same way people see. People look at the outside of a person, but the Lord looks at the heart."

This verse reminds us that it's one thing to look at the outside of a person, but it's another to see the heart. Your heart is beautiful and precious to God. He treasures it.

It's time to look in the mirror in a new way. Try looking at your reflection and saying something like, "Hey, Gorgeous, it's great to see you again." Hey, don't laugh! Try saying, "You look lovely to God."

Stop comparing your looks and your clothes to those of your friends or supermodels. Instead, try seeing yourself as God does.

The best you is the real you.

MESSAGE TO GOD

God, I guess it's great to have cool clothes, but I want to be cool inside and out. Thanks for taking care of me and knowing what's important to me. Help me be the real me. Amen.

Prayer Starters

God, thank you for creating me just as I am. Here are some cool things about me . . .

Dear God, I feel like an ugly duckling because . . .

God, I can be beautiful inside and out by ...

Dear God, you created me. You look at my heart. You see the real, beautiful me. Thank you. Amen.

Here's what I did to help me feel better about myself ...

Here's what God did to answer my prayer ...

I come from a family of high achievers. My parents both have graduate degrees and my older brother is an athlete and gets all A's. I like school, but I feel like I can't keep up with all the things my parents and my teachers want me to do. I want to succeed, but I have too much to do!

signed,

Under Pressure

MESSAGE TO GOD

God, help! I just can't take on one more thing. I need some time to breathe and everyone wants me to do more. I'm stressed out! Amen.

WHaT wOuld YoU Do?

- ✿ Walk around with headphones on and ignore the world.

- ✿ Hide in your closet.

- ✿ Ask your brother if he can help.

- ✿ Talk to your parents and teachers from your heart.

Lots of kids today feel like they're too busy. Their lives are filled up with long lists of school activities, weekend sports, band concerts, church activities, homework, and friends.

Doing your best is important. Setting goals, like getting A's, is a good thing. However, you need time for playing and for rest, too. There are only so many things you can do in one day. God can help you decide which of your tasks are the most important, and he'll give you strength to get them done. Sometimes we wear ourselves out when we don't recognize our own limitations. We need to rely on God to carry us through our work and responsibilities.

Whenever the demands on your time and your thinking become too much, ask God for some help.

Matthew 11:28, 29 says,

"Come to me, all of you who are tired and have heavy loads, and I will give you rest. Accept my teachings and learn from me, because I am gentle and humble in spirit, and you will find rest for your lives."

Ask God to help you find time for this kind of rest. A quiet retreat to sort things through could be worthwhile. It may be helpful to put on your headphones and tune out—as long as you don't tune out for too long!

Your parents' and teachers' intentions for you are good. However, we each have a pace that works for us, and yours is different from your brother's or anyone else's. If you're overwhelmed, have a serious talk with those who care about you. Share your feelings, but stay open to what they have to say, too. Together, pray for God's help in working out a schedule of responsibilities that is reasonable for you.

God, I'm tired. I need rest. Please help all those around me understand that I am doing the best I can. Thank you. Amen.

Prayer Starters

I have too much to do. Here's a list of things that keep me busy...

God, I'm worried that I won't be as good as my parents expect me to be because...

God, help me do my best at . . .

 God, today I am trying to do things without stress. Thank you for my parents and teachers who care about me. Amen.

What I did about this problem . . .

What God did to help me . . .

What I'm learning about myself . . .

So many things seem unfair and put me in a bad mood. When my sister used my computer game without asking, I blew up. When mom asked me to take out the garbage, it irritated me. When my friend got an award and I didn't, I felt mad about that, too. What is it? I just blow a fuse over the dumbest things.

signed,

Volcanic Temper

God, sometimes
I just don't like anything.
I don't even know why I'm
angry, but I am. I know why
Oscar the Grouch lives in a
garbage can. Maybe he feels
yucky, like I do. Please
help. Amen.

WHat wOuld YoU Do?

- ❁ *Take up boxing lessons with a kangaroo.*
- ❁ *Play the drums.*
- ❁ *Stand on a chair and yell as loud as you can.*

We all blow a fuse now and then. Angry feelings are normal and sometimes right. The part God asks us to think about is how we deal with those feelings. Feeling anger can be OK, but acting out in a hurtful way when you're angry is a problem.

James 1:19, 20 says,
"Always be willing to listen and slow to speak. Do not become angry easily, because anger will not help you live the right kind of life God wants."

Wow! Always is a pretty tough order about anything—especially about listening. Even when you're angry, God wants you to listen to the other side. It's hard to do, but it's a great idea. Imagine what it would be like if you always listened to others and they always listened to you. Cool!

After the command to listen, the Bible tells us how we should speak. Speaking slowly means taking time to think about how we'll respond before we say anything. Keep your lips zipped. Don't let angry, mean words fly out of your mouth. Before you make a sound, make sure what you're going to say will please God.

Since you can't shout at the person who made you angry, let's see if there's a better way to work out angry feelings. Taking up boxing lessons with a kangaroo could be tricky unless you live in Australia, but a good punching bag could be great. Playing drums lets you pound on something and be loud which might make you feel better.

Good ways to let off steam
1. Do some exercise.
2. Walk the dog.
3. Organize something.
4. Pray.

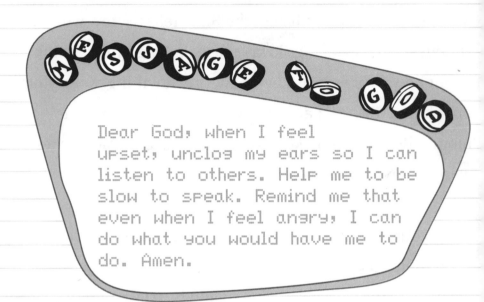

MESSAGE TO GOD

Dear God, when I feel upset, unclog my ears so I can listen to others. Help me to be slow to speak. Remind me that even when I feel angry, I can do what you would have me to do. Amen.

Prayer Starters

God, I'm mad and that's all there is to it! Please help me to ...

God, I'm ready to scream about ...

God, instead of being unkind I'm going to . . .

God, today I will listen to what others say even if I have a different opinion. I will think hard about what I say back to them. I want to live the way you want me to. Amen.

What I did to get over feeling angry . . .

What God did in answer to my prayer . . .

I'm learning more about myself and I like who I am! Sometimes I feel like my friends want to change me because I like different things than they do. I like being quiet and doing my own stuff sometimes, and I like being with friends or my family other times. Isn't it OK to be who I am?

signed,

Me, Myself, and I

MESSAGE TO GOD

Dear God, thanks for creating me and for being with me all the time. I know you "get" who I am. Please help me be myself. Amen.

WHaT wOuld YoU Do?

✿ Ignore everyone who doesn't think like you.

✿ Pretend to be like everyone else.

✿ Only talk to your cat.

✿ Keep trying to be yourself.

Psalm 139:14-16 says,

"I praise you because you made me in an amazing and wonderful way. What you have done is wonderful. I know this very well. You saw my bones being formed as I took shape in my mother's body. When I was put together there, you saw my body as it was formed. All the days planned for me were written in your book before I was one day old."

God knew you before you were even born and he knows you now. What a wonderful thing to know! God made you just as you are—his amazing and wonderful creation. Being you is very important. The verses also say that God even planned all the days of your life. What you do with each of those days is very important.

One of the challenges of growing up is figuring out just who you are. As you grow, you learn more about the person God has designed you to be. What kind of person is God shaping you to be?

If you pretend to be like everyone else, you may stop being yourself. That's not a good choice. God created you on purpose. He knew what he was doing. The best thing to do is simply be yourself—your best self.

You are a perfect creation of God, blessed with special gifts. Don't waste that by giving in to what other people want you to be.

MESSAGE TO GOD

Dear God, thank you for being with me even before I was born. I know you have many wonderful things planned for my life. Please help me figure out who you want me to be. Amen.

Prayer Starters

God, thanks for the many good things in my life like ...

God, I just want to thank you for making me. Here's what I like about myself...

God, help me when I forget to be myself . . .

God, I am trying to be the best me I can be. Thanks for creating me. Amen.

Here are some ways I like being myself . . .

Here are some things God might have planned for me . . .

Cool books for tweens!

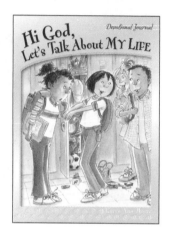

Hi God, Let's Talk About MY Life
Devotional Journal
written by Karen Ann Moore
0-7847-1246-8

Dear God, Let's Talk About YOU
Devotional Journal
written by Karen Ann Moore
0-7847-1247-6

Believe It!
Bible basics that won't break your brain
written by Steven James
0-7847-1393-6

Available now at your local bookstore!